COLLABORATIVE BARGAINING

Training and Reference Manual

Doc Dengenis

Bargaining Training and Strategy Consultant

Champ Publications

Second Edition

March 2014

DEDICATION

This book is dedicated to my beloved children Petra Dengenis Roberts, Rhyne Champ Dengenis, Brig Buswell Dengenis and my grandson, Burton Bailey Roberts.

This book is also for the outstanding teachers and coaches who had a strong influence on my life, Frank D'Amato and Felix Karsky of Bulkeley High School, Joe Beidler, Nutmeg Bowl Coach and Linfield Connection, and finally the Linfield Family James T. Hart (Economics), Colleen Anderson (Creative Writing), and Paul Durham (Football), Earl Milligan (English Composition and World Literature), all late of the great Linfield College Faculty.

TABLE OF CONTENTS

PREFACE

Collaborative Bargaining explains the key foundations of the collaborative/interest-based bargaining process. This is a valuable resource document for all bargainers, regardless of style preference, skill level, or experience. There are new tools to be learned that will be useful in strengthening negotiators' skill sets in any overall bargaining setting. The terms "collaborative" and "interest-based" bargaining will be used interchangeably. There are some valuable skills and strategies to be learned by traditional bargainers; especially at closure when Parties are deadlocked and entrenched in their positions and need creative options in order to achieve settlement. The book will cover advanced skills, sufficient consensus, building an interest-based blueprint, discovery skills, techniques and strategies in interest-based bargaining, and analysis. Participants will have the opportunity to practice skills, techniques, and strategies using education and community issues in exploring and developing bargaining strategies through bargaining simulations and hands-on exercises.

ACKNOWLEDGMENTS

Brig Dengenis provided computer expertise and advice pertinent to the successful completion of *Collaborative Bargaining Training and Reference Manual.* Odis Avritt was responsible for the photo on the back cover. Kristen Hall-Geisler provided valuable copy edit services. The front and back cover designs were created and designed with the help and expertise of Brig Dengenis.

LIFE

Life is complicated with an interesting mix of pure joy and unmitigated disaster. I have experienced great appointments and recovered from serious disappointments. I celebrate with my longtime close personal friends and family the successful completion and self-publishing of my third book, *Collaborative Bargaining Training and Reference Manual.* A wise experienced person told me, "If it hurts, it will make you strong!" I have experienced serious hurt several times during my lifetime, and the statement is true.

Important Reading References

*Fisher, Roger, and William Ury. *Getting to Yes, Negotiating Without Giving In.* New York: Penguin, 1983.

*Ury, William. *Getting Past No.* New York: Bantam Books, 1991.

*Brown, Scott. *Getting Together.* New York: Penguin Books, 1988.

Gerstein, Arnold, and James Reagan. *Win-Win, Approaches to Conflict Resolution.* Salt Lake City: Peregrine Smith, 1986.

Jandt, Fred E. *Win-Win Negotiating, Turning Conflict into Agreement.* New York: John Wiley & Sons, 1985.

Reck, Ross R., and Brian G. Long. *The Win-Win Negotiator.* Escondido, California: Blanchard Training and Development, 1985.

*The Big Three" listed at the top are from my experience the most important reading sources.

Books by Doc Dengenis

Bargaining Essentials. Portland, Oregon: Wildcat-Lava Bear Publishing, 2009.

Advocacy Establishment of Rights. Portland, Oregon: Wildcat-Lava Bear Publishing, 2010.

Dengenis Family History. Seattle, Washington: Champ Publications, 2014.

TRAINING TEAM ROSTER

Staff:
Preparation/Caucus Room:
District/D'Amato
1.
    A.
    B.
    C.
    D.

Bargaining Room:
Preparation/Caucus Room:
Association/O'Brien
2.
    A.
    B.
    C.
    D.

Staff:
Preparation/Caucus Room:
District/D'Amato
3.
    A.
    B.
    C.
    D.

Bargaining Room:
Preparation/Caucus Room:
Association/O'Brien
4.
    A.
    B.
    C.
    D.

Staff:
Preparation/Caucus Room:
District/D'Amato
5.
    A.
    B.
    C.
    D.

Bargaining Room:
Preparation/Caucus Room:
Association/O'Brien
6.
    A.
    B.
    C.
    D.

FACILITIES LIST

1.   One big training room with sufficient tables for a maximum of 4 trainees per table.

2.   Flip chart(s)

Also

1.   Name tags.

2.   Large felt-tip pens

3.   Tape

4.   Parking lot sheet(s).

5.   Certificates.

6.   Rewards.

PREFERABLE ROOM ARRANGEMENT
(Tables chevron-style below)

Flipchart   **Podium**   **Trainers Table**

   X   X   X   X

X   X   X   X   X   X

    X   X

   X   X   X   X   X

X   X   X   X   X   X

    X

PARKING LOT

INTRODUCTION

1. Targeted audience.

2. Prerequisites.

3. Starting and finishing times.

4. General overview of training.

5. Introduce trainers and brief background.

ICE BREAKER

Instructions: Prepare to answer:

A. My name is

_____

_____ .

B. My bargaining experience is_____

_____

_____ .

C.   I was born in the city of_____, state _____ .

D. I live in the city/town of_____ .

E.   My main responsibility at work
is_____

_____ .

F.   My expectations
are_____

_____ .

A Brief Overview of Collective Bargaining in Public Education

18TH Century

The Society of Associated Teachers of New York City was organized in 1794.

19TH Century

1. Thirty state associations were formed between 1845 and 1861.
2. The National Education Association (NEA) was organized in 1857.

20TH Century

1. The Eau Clair (Wisconsin) Federation of Teachers bargained the first teacher collective bargaining agreement in 1941.
2. The Norwalk Teachers Association of Connecticut went on strike to gain recognition in 1946.
3. Wisconsin passed the first state collective bargaining law in 1959 specifically for public school employees.
4. The NEA endorsed "Professional Negotiations" for teachers on 1960.
5. Connecticut, Massachusetts, and Michigan passed public employees bargaining laws in 1965.
6. Hawaii and Pennsylvania legalized the right of public employees to strike in 1970.
7. By 1972, there were 3,911 school systems engaged in collective bargaining.
8. Washington State enacted an agency shop (union security) law for public employees in 1973.
9. The U.S. Supreme Court ruled the NEA was a union in 1979.
10. The NEA was the largest employee organization by 1985.

The Relationship of Power and Bargaining

1. A bargaining relationship is based on power, both real and perceived.
2. If your team does not have power when it goes to the table, the team will not find it there.
3. A team can potentially lose power at the table if there is a fundamental change in the distribution of power negotiated between the Parties.
4. In the event there is a long standing, clear, unbroken past practice, the team should not introduce any issue at the table unless it is ready to go to war to preserve it.
5. In the event a team takes an issue to the table and does not succeed in bargaining it into the contract, then it is lost.

Ways to Get to the "Promised Land/Settlement" in Bargaining (Tools)*

1. Traditional/ Positional Bargaining
2. Collaborative or Interest-Based Bargaining
3. Win-Win
4. Mutual Gains
5. Other creative ways and combinations

* There is no one "right" way to bargain, since any one of the above mentioned or a creative combination can be successful, depending on the Parties.

Different "Looks" for Collaborative Bargaining*

1. Facilitated
2. Self-Managed
3. Co-Facilitated, neutral facilitators or advocate co-facilitators
4. Time Certain "Win-Win" with a marathon weekend and an absolute deadline.
5. Extensive use of subcommittees

* There is nothing "pure" in terms of style. We all bargain everyday over a variety of issues with friends, family, and workers. We use different styles and approaches, depending on whom we are trying to reach a decision. No two bargaining experiences are the same. Styles and processes vary from contract to contract because they are influenced by history, players, and other forces blended into the core of the bargain. Our responsibility is to find a way to weave through these forces and achieve a fair settlement. Individual bargaining styles evolve through ongoing experiences. Any collaborative methodology is not a cure-all. At times confrontation is inevitable because of difficult issues. These new skills should be integrated into and enhance your knowledge base and skill set.

Different Approaches to Non-Traditional Bargaining

1. No Planning.
2. Extensive Preplanning.
3. BATNA or no BATNA
    Best Alternative to a Negotiated Agreement: what your Party can do without the agreement of the other Party.
4. Organizing or no organizing.
    The role of organizing, including joint and/or filtered communication, especially if the process is used for major "take-backs" or massive contract stripping.
5. The existence of comprehensive ground rules or operating procedures (restrictive or not) or a limited number of any other rules.
6. Objective Standards.

Separating the Bargaining Table and the Work Environment

1. Collaborative style bargaining skills are a means of conducting business at the table.
   a. Interest statements developed.
   b. Parties mutually develop issues.
   c. Contract represents mutually endorsed positions of the Parties.

2. Creating a collaborative culture/climate is essential for success in a broader sense.
   a. Employees have authentic participation with a significant voice in the decision-making process.
   b. The Association and its members are recognized as majority stakeholders and are treated as full partners in the decision-making process.

Collaborative Bargaining Process
Preconditions Essential for Success

1. Partners explore different collaborative processes and mutually endorse one, along with ground rules and operating procedures.
2. Internal and joint training in some type of interest/collaborative bargaining process are extremely important.
3. The Association must be strong and the leadership committed to maintaining a strong contract.
4. Power equalization has been completed and Management must respect and/or fear the Association.
5. The Association's leaders must be ready, willing, and able to organize the members to maintain its power base and at the same time keep a strong contract.
6. The Association is accepted as a full partner in the decision-making process for all major work related issues.
7. The Association team has ample opportunity for preplanning to reduce internal conflict.

8. The Association team has preplanned and completed in the preparation stage some type of bargaining blueprint with goals, guidelines, direction, and other critical needs to be met established by team consensus prior to the first bargaining session. The team should not begin the bargain until some type of blueprint is completed by team consensus.

9. The team must keep focused on satisfying the members' needs (substance) and periodically review the blueprint.

10. The team must utilize "No" and "Dead Space strategy" (not respond or overreact) when appropriate and necessary.

11. The team will capture the essence of the agreements in writing during the process rather than waiting until the end when memories have faded.

12. The Association must communicate in writing to all the members after every session.

13. Management must have demonstrated a track record of a reasonable level of trust, honesty, and integrity absent of game playing, especially about finances, over a period of time.

14. All options being discussed are important.

Collaborative Bargaining Pitfalls to Avoid in Order to Be Successful

1. Use these types of processes to avoid conflict or to please the other Party.
2. Become enamored with any process and lose sight of the substance.
3. Substitute the relationship for the substance.
4. Agree to any major "take-backs" or "rollbacks" to meet the needs of the other Party in order to make them feel good.
5. Allow your team to be exploited or victimized by totally relying on the trustworthiness of the other Party.
6. Be dishonest or deceiving.
7. If it does not feel good, stop and reevaluate the substance and/or the process because it probably is not worthwhile anyway.
8. Lose focus—the bargain is about meeting the needs of the members!

Process Ideas for Creating a New Collaborative Culture

1. The message from the leadership of both Parties must agree to work jointly to create a collaborative culture.
2. Joint Training Phase 1
   a. Who
   b. When
   c. Location
   d. Date(s)
   e. Includes major stakeholders: Executive Board, School Board, Association President, Superintendent, other key administrators (Site and Main Office), and Association Officers
   f. Federal Mediation and Conciliation Service Committee Effectiveness Joint Training
3. Ongoing Joint Training Phase 2
   a. Annual Joint Training
   b. New Folks
   c. Tune-up for experienced leaders
4. This will help both Parties
   a. Walk the Walk
   b. Talk the Talk
   c. Walk the Talk
5. Use the same skill-based joint training for site administrators and association site representatives to further embed collaboration in the culture.

General Tests for a Successful Bargain

1. Procedural Satisfaction. There was a fair and orderly process, along with rules and operating procedures equally and mutually developed with dual ownership, endorsed, and followed that allowed for civil discussion and problem resolution.

2. Substantive Satisfaction. The substantive/content issues introduced by the Parties were satisfactorily addressed and resolved to the satisfaction of both parties. Both parties are satisfied their essential interests have been achieved with specific, realistic, workable terms and conditions with clear and unambiguous language.

3. Psychological Satisfaction. At the end of the process, the Parties felt good about the process and the results. One party is not viewed as a loser.

BARGAINING DEFINED

Bargaining is a process designed to manage conflict and produce a consensus document specifying the wages, hours, and conditions of employment mutually agreed upon by the Parties.

Again, there is no one right way to bargain.*

The nature of bargaining means there will be some conflict, stress, pressure, tension, and disagreement inherent in the process, both at the table and in your caucus. It is unavoidable. People who are unable to cope with these pressures should *not* be on a bargaining team.

*The primary goal of the bargain is to meet our member's needs relating to compensation, hours, and conditions of employment.

CONFLICT

1. There are natural conflicts inherent in employee-employer relations because of the power of management via their Management Rights to direct the workforce.
2. These natural conflicts exist in both traditional and collaborative cultures in the workplace.
3. The key is to manage these conflicts in the workplace, at the bargaining table, and in caucuses.
4. Building and maintaining a collaborative culture takes constant vigilance to ensure the advocacy of our members.
5. Advocacy takes precedent over the relationship because of our "Duty to Fairly Represent" our members.
6. Conflict is inherent in the "Duty to Fairly Represent" our constituents, which requires the Association to completely, fairly, and effectively represent the entire bargaining unit and promote unit interests.

TYPICAL STAGES OF INTEREST-BASED BARGAINNG

1. ESTABLISHING RAPPORT

    A.   Ground rules are established.

    B.   Initial interests are exchanged and analyzed by the Parties, and an overall bargaining strategy is formulated.

    C.   The Parties begin to develop a picture of the priorities and an idea of a mutually endorsed final agreement so there are no surprises.

    D.   Major stakeholders are informed about the interests and are involved in the bargaining process.

    E.   Joint data collection and sharing paves the way for constructive bargaining.

    F.   Establishing a bargaining rhythm at the beginning results in building a solid foundation for positive agreements.

2. IDENTIFYING INTERESTS

    A. The Parties approach the issues in an attempt to identify the interests, needs, and concerns defining their proposals utilizing information gathered in the initial phase.

    B. Each team has the responsibility to identify its interests.

3.   GENERATING OPTIONS

   A.   After interests are identified around an issue, the Parties
        cooperatively generate possible options to address those
        interests.
   B.   Brainstorming is frequently utilized method in this stage.

   C.   Each Party's responsibility is to generate options that address
        its interests.

4.   ESTABLISHING OBJECTIVE STANDARDS

   A.   The Parties agree to independent, objective standards for
        evaluating the potentially acceptable options to resolve an
        issue.
   B.   Typical criteria would include
            1. Laws
            2. Comparability
            3. Common practices
            4. Ability (not willingness) to pay
            5. Viability of the Parties.

5. COMMITING TO AN AGREEMENT

The Parties identify the options that would resolve each issue by
satisfying their interests utilizing objective standards. Details of
remaining options are agreed to and settlement language is finalized so
there is mutual endorsement and the Parties are willing to commit to
settlement. The Agreement produces strong ratification votes from their
constituents.

COMPARISON OF STYLES

INTEREST-BASED BARGAINING	POSITIONAL BARGAINING
BARGAINERS SOLVE PROBLEMS	BARGAINERS ARE ADVERSARIES
THE GOAL IS A MUTUALLY AGREED SOLUTION WITHOUT HOSTILITY AND/OR CONFRONTATION	THE GOAL IS TO WIN WHATEVER THE COST
SEPARATE THE PEOPLE FROM THE PROBLEM ON AN ONGOING BASIS	DEMAND MAJOR CONCESSIONS AS A CONDITION OF SETTLEMENT
BE SOFT ON THE PEOPLE, HARD ON THE ISSUES AND IDEAS	BE HARD ON BOTH THE PROBLEM AND THE PEOPLE
PROCEED INDEPENDENT OF TRUST	DO NOT TRUST OTHERS AT THE TABLE
FOCUS ON NEEDS/INTERESTS	FOCUS ON PROPOSALS/POSITIONS
CREATE OPTIONS FOR MUTUAL GAINS	DEMAND GAINS FOR YOUR PARTY AS A CONDITION OF THE RELATIONSHIP
INSIST ON USING OBJECTIVE CRITERIA	AGRESSIVELY PURSUE YOUR DEMANDS
BRAINSTORM	ARGUE AND CONFRONT
GENERATING OPTIONS	ZERO IN AND INSIST ON DEMANDS

COMPARISON OF STYLES

Accommodation, Compromising, Avoidance

1. Bargainers are friends.

2. The goal is agreement.

3. Concessions are made to cultivate the relationship.

3. Trust others at the table.

4. Be soft on both the people and the problem.

Bargaining Styles
Strengths and Weaknesses

1. Collaboration
 A. The strength is both Parties can win while at the same time improving the work relationship.

 B. The downside is aggressive bargainers view this style, as a sign of weakness, and it can be a slow deliberate process.

2. Avoidance
 A. This can be practical when the issues are minor and one party is clearly more powerful.

 B. The disadvantage is normally the problems are postponed rather than resolved, so no change occurs in the end.

3. Competition
 A. The advantage is it is time efficient and normally results in some degree of victory for the most powerful party at the table.

 B. Bargaining deadlocks are common, eventually resulting in retaliation and escalation, creating major long-term problems with the business relationship.

4. Compromise

A. The upside is this is a commonly accepted style comfortable for most people, since it is regarded as fair, as both sides both win and lose to some degree in the process.

B. The downside is opening positions are often "pie in the sky," since Parties anticipate compromise down the road and frequently are not satisfied with the final agreements.

5. Accommodation

A. To accommodators, the relationship is more important than the issues and agreeing when they believe the other Party is "right," regardless of the consequences.

B. The problem is the potential for big losses on key issues with the ultimate loss of major contract provisions, power, and both team and organizational credibility and strength.

Advantages of Positional Bargaining

1. Parties always know where they are in terms of positions.

2. The more powerful party favors this style, because it normally wins by using organizing pressure.

3. Parties are familiar with the process.

4. Parties are experienced in the tactics, actions, moves, and messages during the process in order to gain the advantage.

Disadvantages of Positional Bargaining

1. Oftentimes there is a clear winner and a clear loser. This sows the seeds for major conflict in the next round of bargaining.

2. The Parties generally are not satisfied with the final Agreement because of the compromises made during the process.

3. This lack of satisfaction causes the relationship to deteriorate in the aftermath since there is tension, chaos, and confusion in the working relationship.

4. At times the organizing pressure and resultant compromise fails to produce the desired settlement for either Party.

PEOPLE ISSUES

1. Bargainers have diverse backgrounds, points of view, and values, sometimes fueled by unpredictable emotions.

2. All bargainers have dual interests in both the substance and the relationship.

3. Separate the issues from the relationship.

4. Recognize and understand the emotions of both Parties.

5. Use a "Dead Space Strategy" (do not respond/kneejerk react) to any emotional speeches and/or venting during the process.

6. Confront people problems.

7. Bargainers are people first.

SUBSTANTIVE ISSUES

1. Salaries/Wages

2. Conditions of Employment

3. Insurance Coverage and Carriers

4. Dates

5. Numbers

6. Other Monetary/Compensation

7. Sequence/Order

TEAM MEMBERS' MAIN REASONS FOR BEING ON THE TEAM

Name _____ Worksite _____

I am on this team because _____

_____

_____

_____

_____

_____

_____

_____

_____

_____

_____

_____

_____.

This is *why* I am on the team _____

_____

_____.

ADVANTAGES OF INTEREST-BASED BARGAINING

1. Creative solutions evolve beneficial to the organization as a whole, so both Parties can win.

2. Durable solutions everyone is motivated to uphold since they were jointly developed.

3. An improved relationship between the Parties that moves decision making away from reliance on power, so Parties can help each other win.

5. Participants are problem solvers using fostering strategies focused on some collaborative problem-solving process.

6. Mutually agreed-upon ground rules can help facilitate agreements.

7. Joint committees can brainstorm new ideas by confronting historical, cultural, and institutional roadblocks.

8. There is a more efficient flow of information.

9. Most importantly, constructive, long-term, durable, systemic change, whether substantive or process, can be better achieved using a collaborative approach.

10. Only important interests are on the table, so the process is not held hostage by minor issues and/or interests.

Disadvantages of Interest-Based Bargaining

1. The tendency to conform to others' demands in order to ingratiate yourself with them or in order to escape or avoid stress.

2. The tendency to collaborate because either the party is more powerful or you desire to please them.

3. Teams rely on the trustworthiness of the other party and create a climate for victimization.

MOST IMPORTANT COMPONENTS OF ANY SUCCESSFUL BARGAIN*

1. Preparation

2. Preparation

3. PREPARATION

* Team preparation before you get to the table is just as important as what happens at the table.

Expectation Sharing

Complete the sentence in any way you so choose.

If by the end of this training I

_____

_____

_____

_____

_____

_____

_____

_____

_____

_____ .

then it will have been a success.

BARGAINING TEAM DECISION MAKING

This process can be used in caucus or with both teams at the table.

Introduction/Background:

1. All team members must agree to a decision-making process before the start of bargaining preparation.

2. Do not change the decision-making process when faced with a difficult decision.

3. Teams need to know when their members are in agreement as to how to proceed or on accepting or rejecting a management offer.

The following is the preferred model for making decisions.

Sufficient Consensus is defined as a meeting of the minds where every member of the team is given the opportunity to participate in the discussion and decision. Everyone may not like the decision, but everyone is willing to live with it and will not undermine or sabotage the decision.

The team has the power to declare sufficient consensus in the event that members continue to be blockers by saying "No" and at the same time do **not** offer **viable** options or alternatives within a reasonable, specified time frame.

31

Efficient Way to Achieve Sufficient Consensus to Save Time and Energy
"Thumb System" "Calling for the Thumbs"

1. Up is yes.

2. Down is no.

3. Sideways meets minimum requirement necessary.

4. The team should continue discussion and/or proceed with extreme caution in the event more than one person has voted sideways.

5. A "down thumb" requires the "down" member(s) to offer viable alternatives, so it is *not* a veto.

Each team member votes on *every* decision, *every* time—
NO EXCEPTIONS.

Consensus Captain

1. Team selects a member to insure everyone votes on every decision every time.

2. The Captain "calls for the thumbs" when the discussion is finished.

3. Normally, the Consensus Captain is not the scribe.

Teams reach sufficient consensus when:

1. Teams finally agree on a single alternative.

2. Each team member can honestly say:

    - I believe you understand my point of view.

    - I believe I understand your point of view.

    - Whether or not I prefer this decision, I support it:

        — since it was arrived at openly and fairly

        — and it is the best solution at this time.

SUFFICIENT CONSENSUS MEANS:

1. All participants are encouraged to contribute. Participants should view differences as helpful rather than as a hindrance.

2. Anyone can paraphrase an issue.

3. Everyone at the table has an opportunity to describe his/her thoughts/feelings about an interest/issue.

4. Those who continue to disagree may indicate publicly they are willing to go along for an experimental try for a prescribed period of time.

5. All share in the final decision.

SUFFICIENT CONSENSUS DOES NOT MEAN:

1. A unanimous vote.

2. Everyone's first choice.

3. Everyone agrees, only some are in favor just to get the decision carried out.

4. Designed to avoid conflict or to overcome resistance in the short run.

BASIC TENETS OF "VOICE" IN DECISION MAKING

1. The Parties determine the composition and number of representatives from each constituent group.

2. Our members have a seat with authentic participation and a voice in the decision-making process.

3. Our Association selects its own representatives.

4. Our members have an equal or significant (majority) voice in decision making.

5. Our members are present and participate in the final decisions.

6. The decision-making climate is free of fear and intimidation.

7. If a consensus model is used and consensus is reached, all Parties agree to support the decision and work toward implementation.

8. If you are either late or absent, you consent.

9. The process always moves forward and will not be revisited for any anyone or any reason.

10. The first order of business is to agree on a decision-making process, which cannot be changed.

11. Consensus is when all team members agree on a decision.

12. Sufficient consensus is defined as a meeting of the minds when every member of the team is given an opportunity to participate in the discussion and decision. Everyone may not like the decision, but everyone is willing to live with it.

Maslow's Hierarchy of Needs

The late Abraham H. Maslow has provided us with a series of insights into the dynamics of human motivation. He described motivation and its resultant behavior as flowing from internal responses to the basic needs of humans. This view was first presented by Kurt Goldstein (1940); whose research proved a person was motivated primarily by the internal potentialities of his/her own being and the need for these potentialities to be actualized by the self.

Maslow recognized there were a variety of basic human needs that could be arranged in a hierarchy of relative prepotency. This means human needs could be visualized as stacked in layers. The higher needs were only potentially present as motivators and could not be actualized unless the need on the next level below was satisfied. The diagram below may be helpful in clarifying this point.

Each higher need does not become potent as a motivator until the next lower need is satisfied.

Examples

Need for self-actualization	To do what you must do to become fully yourself; to develop your own individuality.
Ego and esteem needs	Respect and liking for self and others; strength competence; freedom and deserved fame.
Love needs	Membership, acceptance, and belonging, feeling loved and wanted.
Safety needs	Protection from physical or psychological threat as well as fear and anxiety; the need for order and structure.
Survival needs	Food, water, shelter, procreation, etc.

Maslow emphasizes that the need for self-actualization is a healthy person's prime motivation. Self-actualization means actualizing one's potential, becoming everything one is capable of becoming.

Use Questioning Techniques

The power of a question is in its requirement of an answer.

Questions, when properly placed or asked, can put you in control of the bargaining dialogue without over-controlling. Questions must be **clean** and **open** to encourage a full response.

The clean, open question helps to create a trusting atmosphere between the Parties for the following reasons:

- Opportunity to answer with freedom and thought.

- Relevance to an interest, issue, problem, or a decision.

- Clear and complete understanding; often brief (12 words or fewer).

- Only one subject, simple and straightforward.

- Encouragement of honest, useful responses free from fear of reprisal.

- Information seeking rather than binding, demanding, trapping, leading, or limiting.

- Helps in resolving a problem.

- Leads in the direction of concrete solutions.

- Provides others an opportunity to articulate new creative thoughts.

- Requires more than a yes or no answer.

The Triplet Questioning Technique

The Triplet Questioning Technique is a basic skill to help you maintain control, get information, and achieve results in bargaining.

The "Triplet" contains three types of questions, each asked as appropriate, to help participants at the table develop complete ideas.

The three types of questions are:

1. Information Seeking—To get facts, ideas, opinions, and feelings by keeping an open mind, asking open-ended questions with "why" or "why not," and having objective discussions. Examples:

    a. What are some possible causes of the staffing problem?

    b. Where have we observed staffing problems occurring during the past year?

    c. When have we observed staffing problems occurring during the past year?

    d. Who is having staffing problems?

    e. Which of these three alternative solutions do you prefer?

2. Clarifying—To clarify the responses to Information Seeking questions. Examples:

a. When you say, "Seniority interferes with optimal staffing," what do you have in mind?

b. What are some examples of this "administrative nightmare," as you see it?

c. What do you mean when you say, "Principals need greater flexibility"?

3. Justifying—getting the rationale for the responses to Information Seeking questions. Examples:

a. What are some reasons why "letting principals make s selection" would solve your staffing problems?

b. In what ways do you see eliminating seniority as helping to solve the staffing problems?

c. How might "principal selection" contribute to improved staffing?

d. Why do you believe "seniority hurts quality staffing"?

Triplet Questioning Practice Exercise

Now it is time to use this questioning technique.

Remember, three types of questions are important because there are three types of information you wish to gather.

The initial question, which generally begins with the word "what," identifies the information area.

The second question assures you understand the person's answer. You can often begin the second question with: "When you say _____, what do you mean?"

The third question asks the person to explain why they have given the answer. The third question may often begin with, "Why do you think _____ is _____?"

For instance, if Management were planning to limit personal leave days, you might ask, "What are the problems with the current use of personal leave?"

You might get the answer, "Too many people take leave before and after holidays."

Now, "too many people" can mean a lot of different things, so you might ask, "When you say 'too many people,' what do you mean?"

You might get the answer, "We are not able to get enough subs to cover, so we have a problem."

You have thereby unearthed what is probably the real reason the personal leave issue was raised. It is a substitute problem—not a personal leave problem. You probably want to follow up with some additional questions about substitutes. It is likely an opportunity to start a discussion about making the substitute life more attractive.

Often people contribute the clarification and/or justification right in their first answer. Do not mindlessly pursue questions. Use the question(s) that will provide additional information desired.

First, fill in the clarifying question you might ask to follow-up the dialog begun below:

"What should we do to increase member involvement?"

"We should initiate a strong buddy system."

_____

_____

Second, fill in the justifying question to follow-up the dialog begun below:

"What benefits do you get from asking open-ended questions?"

"You get more information from the person who answers."

"When you say 'more information,' what do you mean?"

"I mean people cannot just answer 'yes' or 'no,' so they have to reveal some information, which they originate."

_____

_____

Think about a topic you would like some information on from your colleague because you are going to practice in pairs.

Remember your first question should be short, specific, relevant, and open.

You really cannot formulate your second question until the first has been answered. You can, however, prepare with the standard question openers.

"What ..." (for information).

"When you say, what do you mean?" (For clarification).

"Why ... " (for justification).

As a partner, you can help in this practice by withholding the clarification and justification from your answer to the first question. This may be awkward, but do not give up. If you need some assistance, please call upon your trainers.

Questioning Evaluation Form

Name of Questioner_____.

1. Did the questioner ask an
   information-seeking question?   ☐ yes   ☐ no

   a. Was it open-ended?   ☐ yes   ☐ no

   b. Was it brief (12 words or fewer)?   ☐ yes   ☐ no

   c. One subject?   ☐ yes   ☐ no

   d. Not trapping or limiting, but allowing for
      an open response?   ☐ yes   ☐ no

Comments: _____

_____.

2. Did the questioner ask a
   clarifying question?   ☐ yes   ☐ no

   a. Did it zero in on some aspect
      of the response?   ☐ yes   ☐ no

   b. Was it clear?   ☐ yes   ☐ no

Comments: _____

_____.

3. Finally, did the questioner ask a
   justifying question?   ☐ yes ☐ no

   a. Did it connect back to the
      information seeking question?   ☐ yes ☐ no

   b. Was it simple and clear?   ☐ yes ☐ no

   Comments: _____

   _____

   _____

   _____

   _____

   _____

   _____.

Interests, Issues, Positions, Options, Standards, Contract

1. *Interests:* Interests are the basic motivations, concerns, and needs of people and organizations such as values, principles, reputation, self-esteem, sense of security, sense of belonging, economic well being, recognition, and control over one's life. These are examples of what you want from the bargain and can be satisfied in more than one way.

Interests are:

> rarely negotiable
> usually intangible
> and may be substituted by one or more other interests
> (economic security for time).

2. *Issues:* Issues are the tangible items necessary to acquire, perpetuate, or protect in order to satisfy interests. The need or desire to satisfy interests defines what the issues will be.

Issues are:

> normally negotiable
> usually tangible
> normally measurable, *either* quantitatively or
> qualitatively.

3. ***Position:*** A relative standing or point of view adopted and held at a particular time on an issue. Also, this is your preferred solution to a problem and usually can only be satisfied in one way. These are your demands and specifics your Party wants or what your Party will or will not do.

4. ***Options:*** Potential solutions or parts of a solution that require mutual agreement of the Parties.

5. ***Standards:*** Objective criteria useful in measuring a fair agreement, like industry or area standard, Consumer Price Index, legal ruling or precedent, total monetary compensation.

6. ***Contract/Agreement:*** The mutually endorsed positions of the Parties.

Options

Options are the potential solutions that require the mutual agreement of the Parties.

Interest-Based Approach	Traditional Bargaining
1. Brainstorming	Arguing
2. Generating	Winnowing
3. Seek best solution	Pass judgment
4. Open to new solutions	Stuck on a position
5. Suspending judgment	Analyzing and Evaluating

How to Identify Interests

1. The most powerful interests are basic human needs:
   - Survival
   - Security
   - Economic/financial well being
   - Sense of belonging
   - Recognition
   - Control over one's life.

5. Talk about interests: The purpose of negotiating is to serve your interests.

6. Three types of interests
   a. Shared
   b. Opposing
   c. Differing

   It is easier to resolve interests than positions. All interests introduced are legitimate.

Clarifying Interests

1. Start with an open mind.
2. Ask open-ended questions for information.
3. Start dialogue with "why" or "why not."
4. Lead with "can we try this approach/idea for a period of time?"
5. Discuss and consider the subject objectively.

Interests Identified
For
Local Education Association

1. Economic security for employees.

2. A safe and secure work environment.

3. Positive teaching, learning, and work environment.

4. Professional respect, recognition, and participation of employees as educational partners.

Interest-Based Bargaining Components Relationship and Analysis Between Interests, Issues, and Positions

1. Interest Concept—Financial Security

   A. Interest Statement

   The Association interest is financial security for all members.

   B. Issues

   Salary/wage increase

   C. Positions

   1. Goal or preferred position

   A 10 percent overall increase (generally not presented initially at the table as part of interest-based approach).

   2. Settlement Standard

   An 8 percent overall increase.

   3. Opening Position, if requested.

   A 15 percent overall increase

2. Interest Concept—Time to conduct Association business

A. Interest Statement
The Association needs workday time to efficiently and effectively conduct Association business.
B. Issues
1.President's Release Time.
2. Association Release Time.
C. Positions
1. One-half time released president paid by Management.
2. A pool of 130 days paid by Management used at the discretion of the Association.
D. Settlement Standards
1. One half time released president.
2. A pool of 100 Association leaves days paid by Management.
E. Opening Positions
1. Full-time released president fully paid by Management.
2. A pool of 130-150 days paid by Management used at the sole discretion of the Association.

ESTABLISHING BARGAINING INTERESTS AND ISSUES

Interest No. 1

Issues

1.

2.

3.

4.

Interest No. 2

Issues

1.

2.

3.

4.

Interest No. 3

Issues

1.

2.

3.

4.

Interest No. 4

Issues

1.

2.

3.

4.

ESTABLISHING BARGAINING GOALS*, GUIDELINES, DIRECTION, NEEDS TO BE MET, OR PROBLEMS RESOLVED
* <u>Goal: Preferred Outcome</u>

Interest No. 1
Issues List
1.
2.
3.
4.

Interest No. 2
Issues List
1.
2.
3.
4.

Interest No. 3
Issues List
1.
2.
3.
4.

Interest No. 4
Issues List
1.
2.
3.
4.

ISSUE RATING
BARGAINING ANALYSIS

#1 Rated Issues (Most Important)	#2 Rated Issues	#3 Rated (Least Important)
1)	1)	1)
2)	2)	2)
3)	3)	3)
4)	4)	4)
5)	5)	5)
6)	6)	6)
7)	7)	7)
8)	8)	8)

Interest-Based Worksheet by Teams

1. Interest concept and/or needs statement

   _____

   _____.

2. Issue(s) _____

   _____

   _____

   _____.

3. Problem(s) that must be resolved _____

   _____

   _____

   _____

   _____

   _____.

4. Creative options that would meet our needs __

   _____

   _____

   _____

   _____

   _____

   _____.

Interest-Based Concept Exercise by Teams

1. Interest concept and/or needs statement:

    The Association is a partner in the education process.

2. Identify two issues:

    1. _____

    2. _____

3. Problems that must be resolved for issues in #2:

    A. _____

    B. _____

4. Creative options that would meet our needs:

    _____

    _____

    _____

Interest, Issue, Position, Identification Exercise
Use the team decision-making process

	Concept	(Select One) Identification	(Yes or No) Bargainable
1	Reputation		
2	Money		
3	$10 per hour		
4	Association leave days		
5	Economic well being		
6	10 days Association President leave		
7	Control over one's life		
8	Overtime		
9	$1,000 training for each laid-off employee		
10	Security		
11	Salary		
12	Employees laid off by seniority		
13	Sense of belonging		
14	25 Association leave days		
15	Personal recognition		
16	Safety		
17	Wage		
18	Survival		

Interest, Issue, Position, Identification Exercise*
Use the team decision-making process

	Concept	(Select one) Identification	(Yes or No) Bargainable
19	2 hours for Association Orientation		
20	Belonging		
21	Self-actualization		
22	Feeling loved and wanted		
23	Class Size		
24	Personal leave		
25	Academic freedom		
26	Last and Final Offer		
27	Recognition clause in contract		
28	Financial security		
29	Self-respect		
30	Time		
31	Professionalism		
32	Values		
33	Principles		

* Answers in the Appendix Section at the back of the book.

Preparing (in caucus) Process

- Discuss the situation.
- Determine your method of decision-making (consensus, thumbs, etc.)
- Develop interest concepts.
- Expand each interest concept into an interest statement.
- Write each interest statement at the top of a clean sheet of butcher paper.
- Overlay another sheet of butcher paper below each statement so that you can brainstorm the issues without writing on the original sheet that shows the interest statement.
- Brainstorm the issues within each interest statement.
- Prioritize the issues.
- Brainstorm creative solutions to those issues prioritized.
- Develop a blueprint and sense of what issues must be resolved and what needs must be met for you to have a settlement.

You are now ready to go to the table and do basically the same thing again.

At the Table Process

- Introductions
- Seating arrangements and room/table adjustments. Do you want to sit as "teams" or intermingle your placements? Do you want to have tables or chairs in a circle? Where do you want them?
- Any other preliminaries, timelines, roles, etc.?
- Alternate introducing your interest statements. Discuss shared interests and collapse those that combine together.
- Determine now, if you did not as part of the preliminaries, how you will reach decisions.
- Select an interest to brainstorm issues.
- Decide whether to brainstorm additional interests before working issues on a particular interest or not.
- Clarify issues.
- Advocate, prioritize, and reduce issues. Use questioning techniques.
- Brainstorm creative solutions to issues. Use questioning techniques.
- Jointly agree to solutions.
- Commit to writing and sign agreement.

**Debrief after each session and at settlement.

TEAM ISSUE RATING EXERCISE
Instructions

1. Utilize same team(s), same decision-making process.
2. Rate the issues listed below from #1-#3 and list them under each category by sufficient consensus using the same previous assumptions.

Financial Security	Association Business	Safe/Secure Schools Work Environment
Holidays	Association Leave	Security Guards Materials, Supplies,
Salary/Wage		Equipment Fund
Building Fund for		
Special Needs Students		

#1 Rated Issues
(Most Important)

#2 Rated Issues

3 Rated Issues
(Least Important)

64

ANALYZING PACKAGES IN BARGAINING ISSUES AND/OR PACKAGE ANALYSIS

> *Settlement Scale:*
> +++ resolves problem well
> ++   significant improvement   - minor loss
> +   some improvement   -- major substantive Loss

Issue
Final Agreement   Problem to be resolved   Analysis

1.

2.

3.

4.

5.

6.

7.

8.

TEAM PACKAGE ANALYSIS EXERCISE

Settlement Scale: **+++** resolves problem well
++ significant improvement   **-** minor loss
+ some improvement **--** major substantive loss

Issue	Existing Contract	Problem	Proposed Solution	Analysis (+++,++,+,--)
Interest: Safe/Secure Schools				
1. Guns/Weapons	silent	students continue o bring weapons to school	automatic 5 day suspension	
2. Classroom Phones Checkout when needed	one phone for each wing of building	unable to access phones when needed	employees use cell phones	
3. Security Guards	1 for entire district	not visible enough at district office called when necessary	local police	
Interest: Working Conditions				
1. Materials, Supplies, Equipment Fund	$10,000 district wide	teachers buy out of own pockets district wide	$21,500 District Fund	
2. Building Fund for materials	silent	classrooms not equipped with adequate materials	$41.25 per specials needs student for fund	

f

BARGAINING FINAL ANALYSIS WORKSHEET

(+++,++,+,--)

| Problem to be Solved | Settlement | Analysis |

#1 Rated Issues

#2 Rated Issues

Collaborative Bargaining Blueprint

ESTABLISHING BARGAINING GOALS, GUIDELINES, DIRECTION, NEEDS TO BE MET

Goal, Direction, Guideline(s) or Need(s)	Final Settlement	Analysis* (+++, ++, +, - --)

Interest #1
Issues

Interest #2
Issues

Interest #3
Issues

*Settlement scale:

+++	meets goal or creatively meets a need
++	significant improvement
+	some improvement
-	minor loss
--	major substantive loss

BLUEPRINT

The blueprint is an insurance policy in case it is needed.

If the other party proposes a creative solution that is different from the goal but is of equal or greater value and meets the needs, the team makes a decision whether or not to accept using the sufficient consensus decision-making process.

The key is, "Does it satisfy a need?"

EXAMPLES

In a Seattle Education Association bargain, the District did not want a full union security clause in the contract, which had a grandfather clause to exclude certain members from paying mandatory union dues. The collaborate solution was to determine the dollar amount of the grandfathered dues and bargain an equivalent amount of money allocated for association leave days, which was one hundred district paid association leave days at association discretion.

During a strike in Bellingham, Washington, the District refused to bargain class size for special education students. The solution was to create a special needs fund for each work site based on a weighted student formula of special need students to buy materials and hire aides to satisfy other special education student needs at the site.

The same problem about special education class size occurred in the Spokane, Washington School District. The solution was to hire an additional twenty-two new specialists to help relieve the workload problem.

The Parties should start to bargain collectively with one mutually endorsed interest to start the dialogue, build trust, gain momentum and move toward settlement.

Function/Dysfunction

Collaboration Defined:

Collaboration is one or more persons working with others toward the attainment of a mutually agreed on, shared, desirable goal.

Dysfunctional Collaboration: Disadvantages

- Conforming to others' demands in order to ingratiate yourself with them or in to avoid or escape stress.

- Collaborating because the other party is more powerful or you want to please that party.

- Teams rely on the trustworthiness of the other party and establish a climate for victimization.

The Dilemmas of Bargaining

1. Dilemmas of Goal Definition
    • Bargainers must set realistic, attainable goals of what is achievable.

    • Goals set too high may be perceived as unfair and diminish your chances of getting agreements that meet your needs.

    • Goals set too low may result in obtainment of less than otherwise may have been obtained.

    • Goal attainment of one party is directly contingent on the goals of the other party.

2. Dilemmas of Trust
The dilemma revolves around the extent bargainers can trust each other.

    • Completely relying on the trustworthiness of the other party establishes a climate for your victimization.

    • Not believing anything substantially reduces the possibility of settlement.

    • The words or actions of the other party at sometime during the bargain must be accepted as to its true interest, an offer of good faith, the bottom line, its level of resources, etc., if an agreement is to be reached.

    • Ultimately, it is best to try to convince the other party why it is in their interest to accept your position.

3. Dilemmas of Honesty and Openness

- Total honesty at all times on all points makes you vulnerable to exploitation.
- When the other party suspects you are dishonest or being deceptive, it can impede the process.
- Your party must convince the other party your team is being honest with respect to your bargaining positions.
- Finally, your team must find a balance between total openness and complete deception in order to convince the other party of your sincerity without showing all your "hole cards," which can change during the bargain depending on the relative importance of specific issues.
- Testing of openness and honesty by the parties is ongoing during the process and can be like shifting sands.
- Exploitation creates resistance to future accords. (Exploitation breeds resistance and promotes adversity.)

4. Dilemma of Cooperation versus Competition

- Is it wise to bargain a disproportionate share of the resources at the expense of the other Parties' ability to pay in the long run?
- What happens when as a result of your honesty to achieve a fair settlement, your team discovers later they were exploited?
- What happens to the working relationship when one party believes there was exploitation because of cooperation and/or competition?

Bargaining Conflict Management
Concept and Definitions
How People Deal with Conflict

1. Collaboration: One or more persons working with others toward the attainment of mutually agreed on, shared, desirable goals. This is a form of dispute resolution that emphasizes interest satisfaction over issue resolution. Collaboration encompasses the belief the interests of one Party will not be satisfied unless the interests of the other Party are also satisfied. This evenhanded process involves problem solving and integrating.

2. Avoidance: Ignoring or refusing to acknowledge a conflict exists. This strategy involves losing and/or withdrawing or moving away from the other Party.

3. Accommodation: Satisfying the interests of the adversary through accommodation with little or no interest satisfaction to your Party. This strategy means yielding and moving toward the other Party.

4. Competition: A form of conflict behavior that can lead to domination or eventual destruction of one or both Parties. Competition requires one winner, and a loser. Oftentimes the result is conflict and escalation.

5. Compromise: A form of "sharing" between Parties. Compromising implies a degree of "giving in," which, under more favorable circumstances, would be unacceptable. Compromise requires that in order for each Party to win something, each Party would also lose something. Normally this tempers the conflict and results in settlement but does not satisfy the interest. The key ideas are horse-trading, splitting the baby, compromising, and sharing the resources.

Collaborative Strategy

- Reasonably high expectations with clear understanding of problems to be resolved or the needs that must be satisfied in some fashion.

- Separate the people from the problem.

- Focus on interests, not positions.

- Generate creative options for mutual benefits.

- Utilize objective criteria.

- What is your BATNA (best alternative to a negotiated agreement)? What you can do without the agreement of the other Party?

- Objective Standards, benchmarks or criteria that make a settlement ratifiable (fair standards or fair procedures).

INFORMATION IS IMPORTANT
SKILLED BARGAINERS ARE DEEP
LISTENERS

Two General Types of Questions

1. Open-ended: requires an explanation with the purpose of gaining information.
    a. How did you come to that decision?
    b. What was the main idea behind this new approach?
    c. Explain how and why this is fair.
    d. How are other similar organizations resolving this problem?

2. Closed-ended: requires a yes or no answer or generally a very limited response with the purpose of "pinning down," cornering, or limiting the other party.

> ## You manage the table by asking questions in order to gain information to make wise decisions.

The Most Important Parts of Bargaining

1. Ask "what" and "how" questions that seek information.

2. A truly effective bargain involves both parties asking and answering a series of questions.

3. Interest-based bargaining is a structured brainstorming process designed to generate options. It is a process that involves generating options and winnowing them until there is a meeting of the minds on a final option that is committed to writing.

4. Questions are an integral part of the bargaining at closure. An observer at the table should be able to visualize the settlement by listening to the questions and answers of both parties.

5. Listening—"What are your concerns, problems, needs, interests?"

6. Skilled bargainers are deep listeners.

You should work on developing deep listening skills.

Interest-Based Bargaining
Key Questions*

1. What do you need, or what are your needs?

2. What are your needs on these issues?

3. Use questions that either begin with, "How can we find an acceptable option to solve....?" or "What can we do to …?"

4. Use questions that seek information. "What is the total cost of this option?"

5. Use clarifying questions. "Why do you want to close the school?"

6. Use "what if" language:

   A. To verbally explore possible alternatives/options beneficial to both parties.

   B. To discuss possible coupling options of mutual interest that meet the needs of the parties.

   * In a traditional bargaining setting, participants only speak the "team line" rehearsed in caucus and/or in preparation.

Ways to Say "No"
In Collaborative Bargaining*

No language is better than bad language.
Have clear language or have no language.

** 1. Say "no" and make a good faith effort to find an acceptable alternative.

** 2. The team cannot, in good conscience, recommend this proposal to the members.

* 3. If we accept the proposed solution, we are violating our legal obligation to represent the members.

"No" is a *legitimate* response. Usually the "no" response is accompanied by the reason or reasons for saying no. It is all right to say no, and there is no need to apologize or feel bad about using no as a response. We should, however, in good faith try to find an acceptable solution that meets our needs, attains our goals, and/or resolves the problem.

Breaking Deadlocks

1. Step back and rethink options to resolve the problem.

2. Break/fractionate the issue into component parts.

3. Hold a new brainstorming session to explore mutual gains.

4. Reprocess problems using questioning techniques.

5. Reframe and focus on future outcomes.

6. Utilize a "what if" non-binding strategy session.

7. Explore coupling options and/or creative linkages.

8. Explore trading options.

9. Explore new combinations, patterns, forms, and structures.

10. Establish a trial or "cooling off" period.

11. Experiment and/or pilot a program while educating impacted Parties.

11. Recruit neutral outside consultants for new ideas.

12. Reassign the task to a joint task force and create a new text.

13. Form a new subcommittee to collect new data to avoid past problems.

14. Begin new talks from a different point of view.

15. Give others the opportunity to back out of corners and/or save face.

16. Lay the foundation for a one-text proposal.

17. Refocus on original interest and both Parties avoid being stuck on positions.

Creating Independent Standards

Standards are objective criteria
to measure a fair agreement.

1. Approach the bargain as a mutual
   search for independent standards.

2. Use the standards as a tool to
   persuade and/or to protect.

3. Identify the standards appropriate,
   acceptable, and relevant to the time,
   place, and circumstances.

4. Be reasonable and keep an open
   mind.

Standards

1. Comparability.

2. Some established index—CPI.

3. Competing offers in similar workplaces.

4. Established precedent like legal or contract.

5. Total compensation.

Critical Elements of Independent Standards

1. Universally accepted.

2. Relevant.

3. Workable.

4. Legitimate.

5. Enables both Parties to survive.

6. Equally applicable to the Parties.

7. Stand on own merits.

Alternatives
Comparison of Options and Alternatives

OPTIONS	ALTERNATIVES
1. POTENTIAL AGREEMENTS	ACTIONS WITHOUT AN AGREEMENT
2. JOINT ACTIONS	UNILATERAL ACTIONS
3. WITH THE OTHER PARTY	ON YOUR OWN

BATNA
The Best *A*lternative *t*o a *N*egotiated *A*greement

This is the best alternative that will meet your interests in the event there is no agreement.

Sequence

1. Brainstorm a list of alternatives/actions for the organization in the event no agreement is reached.
2. Reach consensus on the best alternative.
3. The BATNA is the measure of success.
4. BATNA shields the team from being tempted to accept a substandard settlement.
5. BATNA shields the team from rejecting an acceptable settlement offer.
6. A viable BATNA enhances the bargaining power of the team.
7. The BATNA is fluid and can change with time and circumstances.
8. Always assess their BATNA.

Generating Alternatives
With Brainstorming

The Rules of Brainstorming:

1. Post rules during brainstorming.

2. All answers are okay.

3. Repetitions are okay.

4. Judging is NOT okay, so focus on likes.

5. Questions are NOT okay.

6. Ideas do NOT imply ownership.

7. Use imagination and be freewheeling.

8. The more ideas the better.

9. The more variety the better.

10. Combine, expand, piggyback, and build on ideas.

In other words, brainstorming can open up the group and permit all ideas to be offered without fear of criticism. During brainstorming, some method should be used to write all ideas, i.e.:

- Use newsprint or poster paper and felt pen so all ideas are in plain view of the teams.

- Invent options to generate a variety of possibilities for mutual gain.

- When brains are exhausted and the storming slows down or stops,
  Ask clarifying questions ... then,
  Provide time for advocating ... and then,

- Use objective criteria to narrow the list ... then,

- Prioritize items for further discussion.

After brainstorming, the teams can look at a number of alternatives and perhaps more quickly reach consensus on the best solution.

Basic Brainstorming Process

1. Brainstorm

2. Clarify

3. Advocate

4. Prioritize and reduce options (winnow)

Rules:

1. One process (step) at a time

2. One content at a time

3. Reporter is strictly a scribe and must relinquish the chair in order to speak

Team Brainstorming Exercise*

Interest Concept

    Safe Work Environment

Needs Statement

    The Employer will provide a safe, secure school environment.

Brainstorm Issues:

1.

2.

3.

4.

5.

6.

7.

8.

9.

10.

* Potential answers in the Appendix Section at the back of the book.

Lessons from Geese

Fact 1

As each goose flaps its wings, it creates an "uplift" for the birds that follow. By flying in a "V" formation, the whole flock adds 71 percent greater flying range than if each bird flew alone.

Lesson

People who share a common direction and sense of community can get where they are going quicker and easier because they are traveling on the thrust of one another.

Fact 2

When a goose falls out of formation, it suddenly feels the drag and resistance of flying alone. It quickly moves back into formation to take advantage of the lifting power of the bird immediately in front of it.

Lesson
If we have as much sense as a goose, we stay in formation with those headed where we want to go. We are willing to accept their help and give our help to others.

Fact 3

When the lead goose tires, it rotates back into the formation and another goose flies to the point position.

Lesson
It pays to take turns doing the hard tasks and sharing leadership. As with geese, people are interdependent on each other's skills, capabilities, and unique arrangements of gifts, talents, or resources.

Fact 4

The geese flying in formation honk to encourage those up front to keep up their speed.

Lesson
We need to make sure our honking is encouraging. In groups where there is encouragement, the production is much greater. The power of encouragement (to stand by one's heart or core values and encourage the heart and core of others) is the quality of honking we seek.

Fact 5

When a goose gets sick, wounded, or shot down, two geese drop out of formation and follow it down to help and protect it. They stay with it until it dies or is able to fly again. Then, they launch out with another formation or catch up with the flock.

Lesson
If we have as much sense as geese, we will stand by each other in difficult times as well as when we are strong.

Source: Ohio Rites of Passage Network, 2749 Woodhill Road, Cleveland, Ohio

K-12
Centennial Case Study
TEAM INSTRUCTIONS
Trainee Simulation No. 1

> The main objective is to practice the training skills and not demonstrate any bad behavior learned from previous bargaining experiences.

---

1. Team should decide on a decision-making process.

2. Team will decide on trainee's roles for players as specified above. Everyone is allowed to speak. Anyone can decline a speaking role.

3. Timeframe

   Two hours of preparation.
   Two hours of simulation with debrief.

4. Training Goal

   Resolve the dispute using interest based bargaining, if possible, within team planning guidelines. Parties should be reasonable, flexible, and bargain in good faith.

5. The objective is to make a reasonable effort to have a "meeting of the minds" with the other team. Utilize KISS approach.

6. Read the background and Case Study No. 1.

7. Follow the sequence outlined on the next page.

Preparing (in caucus)
Process

- Discuss the situation.
- Determine your method of decision-making (consensus, thumbs, etc.).
- Develop interest concepts.
- Expand each interest concept into an interest statement.
- Write each interest statement at the top of a clean sheet of butcher paper.
- Overlay another sheet of butcher paper below each statement so that you can brainstorm the issues without writing on the original interest statement sheet.
- Brainstorm the issues within each interest statement.
- Winnow the issues (prioritize).
- Brainstorm creative solutions to those issues prioritized.
- Develop a blueprint and sense of what issues must be resolved, what needs must be met, in order to reach settlement.

The team is ready to go to the table and follow the same process again.

At the Table Process

- Introductions
- Agree on seating arrangements and room/table adjustments. Do you want to sit as "teams" or intermingle your placements? Do you want to have tables or chairs in a circle? Where do you want them?
- Any other preliminaries, timelines, roles, etc.?
- Alternate introducing your interest statements. Discuss shared interests and collapse those that naturally combine together.
- Determine now, if you did not as part of the preliminaries, how the teams will reach decisions.
- Select an interest to brainstorm issues.
- Decide whether to brainstorm additional interests before working issues on a particular interest or not.
- Clarify issues.
- Advocate, prioritize, and reduce issues. Use questioning techniques.
- Brainstorm creative solutions to issues. Use questioning techniques.
- Jointly agree to solutions.
- Commit to writing and sign agreement.
- Debrief after each session and at settlement.

Basic Brainstorming Process

1. Brainstorm

2. Clarify

3. Advocate

4. Prioritize and reduce options (winnow)

Rules:

1. One process (step) at a time

2. One content at a time

3. Reporter is strictly a scribe and must relinquish the chair in order to speak

K-12
THE CASE OF THE CENTENNIAL SCHOOL DISTRICT
THE CENTENNIAL EDUCATION ASSOCIATION
THE CENTENNIAL COMMUNITY
Simulation #1
Background Paper

Over the past few years there has been a rising tide of guns and weapons on the Centennial School grounds. Employees fear for their lives. There have been student and non-student assaults on the school grounds. Principals and vice principals only appear once or twice for a few minutes to observe teaching during the course of the year because they are handling a mountain of discipline problems on a daily basis. Support staffs oftentimes are expected to watch potentially dangerous students because administrative staff are dealing with discipline problems. Education employees are frightened. Every day gangs roam the hallways during school and the adjacent grounds before and after school. Assaults on students have become commonplace. Last year there were four incidents of assault and battery by students on employees. Guns and weapons are increasingly present on school grounds.

The new superintendent realized drastic measures were necessary in order to revitalize and stabilize the schools. The Board is committed to establishing a safer environment for everyone. Effective schools and a safe environment are interlocked. Hiring additional security personnel with personal communications may be necessary.

There is total agreement that schools are no place for guns and weapons, and harsh measures are necessary to deal with these problems. The employees have demanded additional phones be established in the buildings both for protection and to contact parents immediately about problems. Principals who are concerned about phones being available to employees in classroom and major work areas because the potential for gossiping with spouses and friends could become widespread during the workday are pressuring the School Board. Also, the administrators are concerned about unauthorized long distance phone calls. The Superintendent has encouraged brainstorming by all his charges and the Board to come up with creative solutions.

The District has ample financial resources to adequately create solutions to deal with these problems.

The Association represents both certificated and classified employees. All Parties have agreed to use an interest-based approach to create a plan to effectively alleviate the problem and create a new community friendly school based environment. The teams will be integrated with different community constituents as specified on next page. This blended structure is a radical departure from past practice.

Parties:

CEA Players

1. 1 Association high school representative
2. 1 Association middle school representative
3. 1 Association elementary school representative
4. 1 campus security officer

CSD Players

1. 1 high school assistant principal
2. 1 middle school assistant principal
3. 1 elementary school principal
4. 1 school board member

(Optional Players)*
1. 1 minister
2. 1 Chamber of Commerce
4. 1 PTA member
5. 1 Local police officer

Interest-Based Worksheet by Teams

1. Interest concept and/or needs statement

   _____.

2. Issue(s)_____

   _____

   _____

   _____

   _____.

3. Problem(s) that must be resolved _____

   _____

   _____

   _____

   _____.

4. Creative options to meet overall needs _____

   _____

   _____

   _____

   _____

   _____

   _____.

Interest Based Worksheet by Teams

1. Interest concept and/or needs statement _____

_____ .

2. Issue(s) _____ _

_____ _

_____ _

_____ _

_____ .

3. Problem(s) that must be resolved _____ _

_____ _

_____ _

_____ _

_____ .

4. Creative options to meet overall meet needs _____ _

_____ _

_____

_____

_____

_____

_____

_____

_____ .

AGREEMENTS

Association   Date   Management

TEAM DEBRIEF EXERCISE

> If teams are seated together, some team members should switch places at the table so trainees are seated differently and effectively end the role-playing.

1. What was your team decision-making process? What way did you use to achieve this end?
2. How did your team analyze or track the progress of the bargain?
3. Rate the parties in the bargain on the basis of 1-10 points in each of the following areas (internal/external) within each general category (refer to sufficient consensus section), with 10 points being the best.

	Association Rating Points	District Rating Points
A. Procedural Satisfaction		
1) Internal*	_____	_____
2) External	_____	_____
B. Substantive Satisfaction		
1) Internal	_____	_____
2) External	_____	_____
C. Psychological Satisfaction		
1) Internal	_____	_____
2) External	_____	_____

4. Teams share goals, guidelines, and direction or needs to be met.

5. Teams share settlement analysis results.

6. Was brainstorming utilized? _____

7. Each participant generally shares his/her view of training exercise.

*Internal: own caucus. External: entire bargaining process.

**Observation Form for Staff
Use Only
for Simulation No. 1**

*Have some trainees switch seat placement before debrief if teams have
remained seated together.*

1. List interest concepts or needs statement clearly identified

    A.

    B.

    C.

    D.

2. List issues clearly identified

    CSD   CEA
    A.   A.

    B.   B.

    C.   C.

    D.   D.

3. Problems to be resolved clearly identified in caucus.
   <u>CSD</u>   <u>Problems to be resolved</u>

   A.

   B.

   C.

   D.

   E.

   F.

4. <u>CEA</u>   <u>Problems to be resolved</u>

   A.

   B.

   C.

   D.

   E.

   F.

5. Questions Utilized

	CSD	Yes	No	CEA	Yes	No
a.	Open					
b.	Closed					
c.	What if					
d.	Triplet Clarifyin g Justifying					
e.	Other					
f.						

6. How were decisions made and method used?

A. CSD _____

C. CEA _____

7. Was Blueprint properly developed?

8. Teams briefly explain their blueprint and analyze results.

9. Did the parties engage in a speech and debate exercise or was there meaningful collaborative bargaining taking place? _____

10. Was brainstorming effectively used? _____

THE CASE OF THE BULKELEY SCHOOL DISTRICT AND THE BULKELEY EDUCATION ASSOCIATION
K-12 Simulation #2
Background Paper

The education of the children of the Bulkeley School District, located in a large metropolitan area in "Urbanopolis," is in declining, especially the last five years. Various local governments have provided rhetoric but little to no follow-up or commitment. A new superintendent was selected, and she is committed to cooperate and work with all the educational staff. Also, the School Board has undergone a recent transformation with several progressive members elected. The principals are committed to reform. All the Parties agree the Bulkeley Education Association (BEA) will be a proactive partner rather than a reactive antagonist.

A group of influential parents and powerful business interests have found a group called SOS (Save Our Schools) and organized to successfully pass a substantial levy. In addition SOS solicited significant grant monies from local businesses to save the schools.

The new administration is interested in promoting citizen involvement groups (CIGS) at each school site to make the patrons stakeholders in the decision-making process. Successful schools mean parental involvement. Historically, the parents were alienated from schools because of long-distance central administrative control. The prevailing attitude over the years was, "We know what is best for your children given the financial restraints of the District."

The employees are interested in increasing their involvement in decision-making at their work sites. They are interested in establishing some type of decision-making body, with the employees having a majority voice. Other representatives on the governing body would be one administrator and some parents. These local governing bodies would be responsible for shaping the schools according to the local neighborhood values so all participants believe they have some control over their destiny rather than being dictated to by the central administration.

The Association represents both certificated and classified. Both Parties agree to use interest-based bargaining to resolve the dispute.

Parties:

BSD	BEA
Players	Players
1. Superintendent	1. Association President
2. School Board Chair	2. Paraprofessional President
3. Budget Person	3. Association Chief Bargainer
4. High School Principal	4. Education Employee (Secondary)
5. Middle School Principal	5. Education Employee (Elementary)

Preparing (in caucus)
Process

- Discuss the situation.
- Determine your method of decision-making (consensus, thumbs, etc.).
- Develop interest concepts.
- Expand each interest concept into an interest statement.
- Write each interest statement at the top of a clean sheet of butcher paper.
- Overlay another sheet of butcher paper below each statement so that you can brainstorm the issues without writing on the original interest statement sheet.
- Brainstorm the issues within each interest statement.
- Winnow the issues (prioritize).
- Brainstorm creative solutions to those issues prioritized.
- Develop a blueprint and sense of what issues must be resolved, what needs must be met, in order to reach settlement.

The team is ready to go to the table and repeat the process.

At the Table Process

- Introductions
- Agree on seating arrangements and room/table adjustments. Do you want to sit as "teams" or intermingle your placements? Do you want to have tables or in a circle with chairs? Where do you want them?
- Any other preliminaries, timelines, roles, etc.?
- Alternate introducing your interest statements. Discuss shared interests and collapse those that naturally combine together.
- Determine now, if you did not as part of the preliminaries, how the teams will reach decisions.
- Select an interest to brainstorm issues.
- Decide whether to brainstorm additional interests before working issues on a particular interest or not.
- Clarify issues.
- Advocate, prioritize, and reduce issues. Use questioning techniques.
- Brainstorm creative solutions to issues. Use questioning techniques.
- Jointly agree to solutions.
- Commit to writing and sign agreement.

**Debrief after each session and at settlement.

Basic Brainstorming Process

1. Brainstorm

2. Clarify

3. Advocate

4. Prioritize and reduce options (winnow)

Rules:

1. One process (step) at a time

2. One content at a time

3. Reporter is strictly a scribe and must relinquish the chair in order to speak

Interest-Based Worksheet by Teams

1. Interest concept and/or needs statement

    _____

    _____.

2. Issue(s)_____

    _____

    _____

    _____

    _____.

3. Problem(s) that must be resolved_____

    _____

    _____

    _____

    _____.

4. Creative options to meet overall meet needs

    _____

    _____

    _____

    _____

    _____.

Interest-Based Worksheet by Teams

1. Interest concept and/or needs statement

   _____.

2. Issue(s)_____

   _____

   _____

   _____

   _____.

3. Problem(s) that must be resolved_____

   _____

   _____

   _____

   _____.

4. Creative options to meet overall meet needs

   _____

   _____

   _____

   _____

   _____.

AGREEMENTS

_____   _____   _____
Association   Date   Management

TEAM DEBRIEF EXERCISE

If teams are seated together, some team members should switch places at table so people are seated differently and effectively end the role-playing.

1. What was your team decision-making process? How was it used?

2. How did your team analyze or track the progress of the bargain?

3. Rate the parties in the bargain on the basis of 1-10 points in each of the following areas (internal/external) within each general category (refer to sufficient consensus) with 10 points being the best.

	Association Rating Points	District Rating Points
A. Procedural Satisfaction		
1) Internal*	_____	_____
2) External	_____	_____
B. Substantive Satisfaction		
1) Internal	_____	_____
2) External	_____	_____
C. Psychological Satisfaction		
1) Internal	_____	_____
2) External	_____	_____

4. Teams share goals, guidelines, direction, or needs to be met.

5. Teams share settlement analysis results.

6. Was brainstorming utilized? _____

7. Each participant generally shares his/her view of training exercise.

*Internal: own caucus. External: entire bargaining process

(Have some trainees switch seat placement before debrief if teams have remained seated together.)

1. List interest concepts or needs statement clearly identified.

    A.

    B.

    C.

    D.

2. List issues clearly identified.

    <u>BSD</u>   <u>BEA</u>
    A.   A.

    B.   B.

    C.   C.

    D.   D.

    E.   E.

116

3. Problems to be resolved clearly identified in caucus.

   <u>BSD</u>   <u>Problems to be resolved</u>

   A.

   B.

   C.

   D.

   E.

   F.

4. <u>BEA</u>   <u>Problems to be resolved</u>

   A.

   B.

   C.

   D.

   E.

   F.

5. Questions Utilized

	BSD	Yes	No	BEA	Yes	No
A.	Open					
B.	Closed					
C.	What if					
D.	Triplet Clarifying Justifying					
E.	Other					
F.						

6. How were decisions made and method used?

    A. BSD_____

    B. BEA _____

7. Was the Blueprint properly developed?

8. Teams briefly explain their blueprint and analyze results.

9. Did the parties engage in a speech and debate exercise or was there meaningful collaborative bargaining taking place?_____

10. Was brainstorming effectively used?_____

GENERIC

Case of the Arguing Authors Instructions

The main objective is to practice the training skills and <u>not</u> demonstrate any bad behavior learned from previous bargaining experiences.

1. Select O'Brien Team and D'Amato Team.

    A. O'Brien   A. D'Amato

    B. O'Brien Family   B. D'Amato Family
        Brother and sister   brother and sister
        (One is an attorney,   (one is an attorney,
        One is a tax expert).   One is a tax expert).

2. Timeframe

    A. One hour of preparation.

    B. Approximately 1-1/4 hours of interest based bargaining.

    C. One half hour of debrief with teams.

3. Training Goal
    Resolve the dispute using interest based bargaining, if possible, within team planning guidelines. Parties should be reasonable, flexible, and bargain in good faith.

4. Read Case Study.

5. Follow the sequence on the next page.

Preparing (in caucus) Process

- Discuss the case.
- Determine your method of decision-making (consensus, thumbs, etc.).
- Develop interest concepts.
- Expand each interest concept into an interest statement.
- Write each interest statement at the top of a clean sheet of butcher paper.
- Overlay another sheet of butcher paper below each statement so the team can brainstorm the issues without writing on the original sheet with the interest statement.
- Brainstorm the issues within each interest statement.
- Prioritize the issues.
- Brainstorm creative solutions to those issues already prioritized.
- Develop a blueprint and a sense of what issues must be resolved, what needs must be met, in order to achieve settlement.

The team is ready to go to the table and do basically the same thing again.

At the Table Process

- Introductions
- Seating arrangements and room/table adjustments. Do you want to sit as "teams" or intermingle your placements? Do you want to have tables or a circle of chairs? Where do you want them?
- Any other preliminaries, timelines, roles, etc.?
- Alternate introducing your interest statements. Discuss shared interests and collapse those that easily combine together.
- Determine now, if you did not as part of the preliminaries, how you will reach decisions.
- Select an interest to brainstorm issues.
- Decide whether or not to brainstorm additional interests before working issues on a particular interest.
- Clarify issues.
- Advocate, prioritize, and reduce issues. Use questioning techniques.
- Brainstorm creative solutions to issues. Use questioning techniques.
- Jointly agree to solutions.
- Commit to writing and sign agreement.
- Debrief after each session and at settlement.

Basic Brainstorming Process

1. Brainstorm

2. Clarify

3. Advocate

4. Prioritize and reduce options (winnow)

Rules:

1. One process (step) at a time

2. One content at a time

3. Reporter is strictly a scribe and must relinquish the chair in order to speak.

GENERIC

Trainee Simulation #3

The Case of the Arguing Authors

Pat O'Brien, Ph.D., a middle-aged friend of yours who is a history teacher in the Social Studies Department of a large local, nationally acclaimed high school in a highly visible large metropolitan city, has consulted you about a problem greatly troubling her.

Collaboratively with Chris D'Amato, a younger history teacher at another high school in the same city, she has written a book that is about to be sent out to prospective publishers. D'Amato, a rising professional, has aspirations to be college professor sometime in the near future.

As with any extended collaboration—this one over a period of almost four years—there have been ups and downs in the relations between the two authors, but they managed to resolve their problems. Chris and Pat believe they have produced an important and high-quality high school textbook.

The problem was when it came to doing the title page; there emerged a strong disagreement over whose name should be first. O'Brien believes, as the senior member of the pair (indeed, O'Brien was one of D'Amato's mentors while finishing his dissertation and eventually Ph.D. at Carvard University), she had always taken it for granted that her name would be first. D'Amato, who has already started to write another book, insists that he did the bulk of the work; therefore; his name should be first.

O'Brien now comes to you, as a family member, and asks for advice. "We each see this as a matter of principle, and neither of us will back down. Yet we really must get this matter resolved quickly in order to get this book to prospective publishers. Can you help us resolve this stalemate?"

They have consulted with family members to help resolve the dispute. Both of them attended Carvard University, which is rated consistently in the top ten academic institutions in the country.

O'Brien's children have graduated from college and are pursuing their careers, but she has discussed with the university president the possibility of establishing a fund for scholarships in her family name. She is also a highly respected member of the Board of Regents at the local university.

D'Amato's brother, who is confined to a wheelchair, has just finished computer studies at a local business college. He recently applied for a job at the business office at Carvard. D'Amato has been a family mentor for him over the years and is very concerned about his economic well being.

Both Parties agree to attempt to resolve the dispute using interest based bargaining.

> The main objective is to practice the training skills and not demonstrate any bad behavior learned from previous bargaining experiences

Interest Based Worksheet by Teams

1. Interest concept and/or needs statement

   _____.

2. Issue(s)_____

   _____

   _____

   _____

   _____.

3. Problem(s) that must be resolved_____

   _____

   _____

   _____

   _____.

4. Creative options to meet overall meet needs

   _____

   _____

   _____

   _____.

Interest Based Worksheet by Teams

1. Interest concept and/or needs statement

    _____.

2. Issue(s)_____

    _____

    _____

    _____

    _____.

3. Problem(s) that must be resolved_____

    _____

    _____

    _____

    _____.

4. Creative options to meet overall meet needs

    _____

    _____

    _____

    _____.

AGREEMENTS

Association   Date   Management

TEAM DEBRIEF EXERCISE

> Some team members should switch places at table so people are seated differently and effectively end the role-playing

1. What was your team decision-making process? What way did you use to achieve this end?

2. How did your team analyze or track the progress of the bargain?

3. Rate the parties in the bargain on the basis of 1-10 points in each of the following areas (internal/external) within each general category (refer to sufficient consensus section) with 10 points being the best.

	D'Amato Rating Points	O'Brien Rating Points
A. Procedural Satisfaction		
1) Internal*	_____	_____
2) External*	_____	_____
B. Substantive Satisfaction		
1) Internal	_____	_____
2) External	_____	_____
C. Psychological Satisfaction		
1) Internal	_____	_____
2) External	_____	_____

4. Did each team meet its needs?

5. Was brainstorming utilized?

6. Each participant generally shares his/her view of training exercise.

*Internal: own caucus. External: entire bargaining process

```
Case of Arguing
Authors
Observation Form for
Staff Use
For Generic Simulation
No. 3
```

(Have some trainees switch seat placement before debrief
if teams have remained seated together.)

1. List interest concepts or needs statement clearly
   identified.

   A.

   B.

   C.

   D.

2. List issues clearly identified.

<table>
<tr><td>O'Brien</td><td>D'Amato</td></tr>
<tr><td>A.</td><td>A.</td></tr>
<tr><td>B.</td><td>B.</td></tr>
<tr><td>C.</td><td>C.</td></tr>
<tr><td>D.</td><td>D.</td></tr>
<tr><td>E.</td><td>E.</td></tr>
<tr><td>F.</td><td>F.</td></tr>
</table>

3. Problems to be resolved clearly identified in caucus.

<table>
<tr><td>O'Brien</td><td>Problems to be resolved</td></tr>
<tr><td>A.</td><td></td></tr>
<tr><td>B.</td><td></td></tr>
<tr><td>C.</td><td></td></tr>
<tr><td>D.</td><td></td></tr>
</table>

E.

F.

4. <u>D'Amato</u>   <u>Problems to be resolved</u>

A.

B.

C.

D.

E.

F.

5. Questions Utilized

	D'Amato	Yes	No	O'Brien	Yes	No
A	Open					
B	Closed					
C	What if					
D	Triplet Clarifying Justifying					
E	Other					
F						

6. How were decisions made and method used?

A. D'Amato _____

B. O'Brien _____

7. Was Blueprint properly developed?

_____

8. Teams briefly explain their blueprint and analyze results.

9. Did the parties engage in a speech and debate exercise or was there meaningful collaborative bargaining taking place?_____

10. Was brainstorming effectively used?_____

Evaluation

1. The most significant part of the training was:

2. The best parts of this training were:

3. Suggestions for improvement are:

FINAL TOTAL GROUP

DEBRIEFING
COMMENTS/OBSERVATIONS

1.Essentials of Bargaining and Advocacy Books are available from the author, Doc Dengenis.

2.   The most important work is done before you get to the table.

3.   Brainstorming

4.   Sufficient consensus

5.   Interests, Issues, Positions

6.   Triplet and other questioning techniques

7.   Clearly outline all problems that must be resolved.

8.   Settlement analysis and tracking instrument

9.   Any other comments, questions, reactions

FINAL TRAINEE WRITTEN EVALUATION

1. What is your reaction to this training in general?

2. What was most helpful about the training?

3. What would you have changed?

4. What would you like to know more about?

Comments/Suggestions (use back, if necessary)

Epilogue
The Rise and fall of Collaborative Bargaining

The first interest-based bargaining discussions and training I was involved in started in 1980 in Washington State with Bill Lincoln. The Washington Education Association (WEA) was a learning organization and open to new ideas and training. Lincoln earned his "bones" as a hostage release negotiator in the prison system. Some staff embraced the new bargaining process, while others viewed it as a soft approach to negotiations. The staff was split, and it was one of the sparks that touched off a long-simmering staff war, along with the accompanying mistrust and organizational paralysis.

WEA Management was supportive of the new style, and those who preferred the traditional style were labeled "dinosaurs." Some of the resultant collaborative bargaining settlements I reviewed were filled with meaningless words and philosophical statements with absolutely no substance. The process worked in some school districts and failed in others, resulting in strikes, depending on the skill set of the major players at and away from the table, bargaining parameters of the Parties, and the existing local culture.

The public sector education labor front was full of strikes and turmoil in the 1970s and early 1980s because of long-simmering tensions and lack of voice over daily working conditions. Associations created lofty expectations with pie in the sky opening positions backed up with strong effective local membership organizing activities. This shifted the balance of power at the table by demonstrating new muscle and resultant power by keeping management off balance using divide and conquer tactics and forging AAA+ Association settlements at the expense of Management. Some of these settlements could have been signed on the decks of the USS Missouri. Saul Alinsky tactics were prevalent as staff became familiar with his books.

Over the next several years, educational employees experienced declining resources, control over salaries and benefits by state legislatures, erosion of confidence in public schools, the birth of charter schools, rising enrollments in private schools, increasing popularity of home schooling, and in general union bashing. In this setting, non-traditional bargaining was popular. The new pressures from organizations like the National Education Association, etc., constituents, and society in general led to the rise in popularity of non-traditional bargaining processes. The trend was to abandon the traditional approaches and move to more collaborative bargaining approaches with problem solving at its core.

In the 1990s and beyond, the Parties have reverted to more traditional approaches, especially with Management resorting to layoffs and take-backs on key financial issues in order to cope with major losses of state and local funding. Trying to successfully collaborate and attempting to roll back major provisions from contracts are not compatible at the bargaining table in my experience.

The Wisconsin public sector labor faceoff in 2011 will result in class warfare soon because of workers' loss of voice in their work life. This is union busting, not even thinly disguised, in a historically progressive state with a rich and storied labor history. I believe the working folks and liberals in the country will rise to the occasion and fight back strong to stop this attempt to disenfranchise the working people and turn the USA into a third-world nation. The next several years will be rich with labor–management and government–labor strife for power, both at the bargaining table and the legislative arenas.

These attempts at union busting by conservative groups will make middle-class working folks stronger in the immediate future.

Appendices

Collaborative/Interest-Based Bargaining Registration Form

Local Association _____

Participants: _____

Name _____ Phone _____

Years of Bargaining Experience _____

Name _____ Phone _____

Years of Bargaining Experience _____

Name _____ Phone _____

Years of Bargaining Experience _____

Name _____ Phone _____

Years of Bargaining Experience _____

Name _____ Phone _____

Years of Bargaining Experience _____

Name _____ Phone _____

Years of Bargaining Experience _____

Form due by:_____

Return to:_____

ATTENDANCE SHEET

BARGAINING TRAINING

SIGN IN   **DATE**

_____   _____

_____   _____

_____   _____

_____   _____

_____   _____

_____   _____

_____   _____

_____   _____

INTEREST, ISSUE, POSITION, IDENTIFICATION EXERCISE
using a team decision-making process

	Concept	(which one) Identification	(yes or no) Bargainable
1	Reputation	interest	no
2	Money	issue	yes
3	$10 per hour	position	yes
4	Association leave days	issue	yes
5	Economic well-being	interest	no
6	10 days Association President leave	position	yes
7	Control over one's life	interest	no
8	Overtime	issue	yes
9	$1,000 training for each laid-off employee	position	yes
10	Security	interest	no
11	Salary	issue	yes
12	Employees laid off by seniority	position	yes
13	Sense of belonging	interest	no
14	25 Association leave days	position	yes
15	Personal recognition	interest	no
16	Safety	interest	no
17	Wage	issue	yes

INTEREST, ISSUE, POSITION, IDENTIFICATION EXERCISE
using a team decision-making process

	Concept	(which one) Identification	(yes or no) Bargainable
18	Survival	interest	no
19	2 hours for Association Orientation	position	yes
20	Belonging	interest	no
21	Self-actualization	interest	no
22	Feeling loved and wanted	interest	no
23	Class size	issue	yes
24	Personal leave	issue	yes
25	Academic freedom	issue	yes
26	Last and Final Offer	position	yes
27	Recognition clause in contract	issue	yes
28	Financial security	interest	no
29	Self-respect	interest	no
30	Time	interest	no
31	Professionalism	interest	no
32	Values	interest	no
33	Principles	interest	no

=

Team Brainstorming Modeling Exercise
Potential Issues (Answers to Brainstorming)

1.   Assault on Employees/Special Assault Leave not out of sick leave.

2. Assaults on Students

3.   Guns/Weapons

4.   Student Discipline

5.   Classroom Phones

6.   Classroom Intercoms

7.   Security Personnel

8.   Drugs in Schools

9.   Alcohol in Schools

10.   Employee Protection
     A.   Liability Insurance
     B.   Legal Defense
     C.   Disability - no loss of pay
     D.   Personal Property Protection

11.   Leave Sharing

12.   Vandalism Fund

13.   Safe Working Conditions

14.   Staff informed of deviant behaviors of new students

15. Reasonable measures to protect oneself

16. Not required to search students, their possessions, or lockers.

Bargaining Realities

1. The team is trying to fulfill the member needs identified and agreed to through a consensus process in the blueprint-planning document developed prior to the bargain.

2. Member backing of the issues and the team is essential.

3. Communication with the membership is key regardless of the bargaining style used at the table.

4. Sometimes a big win is not losing anything.

5. Bargaining is an ongoing, never-ending process.

6. Bargaining happens away from the table at times.

7. Key issues often are resolved at late in the bargain.

8. All team members must reveal upfront their key issues and why they are on the team, so there are no surprises at closure.

9. The day-to-day working relationship with the other Party will likely be the same at the table.

10.   Bargaining is part science (knowing how to build a plan that will result in a fair deal) and part art (knowing how to forge a deal), timing, taking advantage of opportunities, and knowing when and how to close.

11.The use of outside advisors/attorneys normally means trouble. Attorneys are trained in the law. Employee contract bargaining deals with compensation, hours, and working conditions with a Conformity to Law clause, so having an attorney is no advantage.

Dysfunctional Bargainers

Tom Treason - agrees with proposal, strategy, or settlement up front, then immediately seeks to undermine everything afterward.

Ann Absent - sporadic attendance at meetings or bargaining sessions and continually wants to redo everything missed.

Mabel Mouthy – skilled in filibuster, deaf ears, could talk handles off doors.

Ned Negative – a typical contrarian, and his answer is always, "No!"

Ann Affirmation - it matters not what the other party offers; the answer is always yes—because her spouse is on the other team.

Bob Blabber - discloses everything and anything about team strategy, goals, and information.

Ginny Grinder - one issue with an ax to grind and no real interest in any other issue by either Party.

Sam Space - present in body only, never participates, lives in stratosphere. Tunes in every once in a while and asks, "Are we there yet?"

Sandra Signal- telegraphs everything with body language.

Alex Accommodate – makes the other party aware he agrees with their positions on all key issues, since his supervisor is sitting across the table and he is trying to get his job upgraded in classification to make more money.

Contact information:

Doc Dengenis

Bargaining Training and Strategy Consultant

9023 Mary Ave NW
#100
Seattle, WA 98117

www.dengenisconsulting.com

docdengenis@gmail.com

503.803.4229

Made in the USA
Middletown, DE
23 March 2018